Morning Buds

An Anthology of Young Writers

ISBN 978-93-5559-142-5

Published in India 2021 by Pencil

Contributors:
Co-Author: Taukir Suhan
Co-Author: Rochishnu Majumder
Co-Author: Arghadeep Das
Co-Author: Rishav Mitra
Co-Author: Subarno Sen

A brand of
One Point Six Technologies Pvt. Ltd.
123, Building J2, Shram Seva Premises,
Wadala Truck Terminal, Wadala (E)
Mumbai 400037, Maharashtra, INDIA
E connect@thepencilapp.com
W www.thepencilapp.com

DISCLAIMER: *The opinions expressed in this book are those of the authors and do not purport to reflect the views of the Publisher.*

Author biography

The group of authors writing these exceptional pieces of prose and poetry are eighth and ninth grade students of a reputed English medium school from Kolkata, with a penchant for expressing themselves in beautiful words. They came together as an online group called Teen English which has since then been discontinued. However, their writing remains a habit and a hobby.

CONTENTS

Foreword

Every beginning is beautiful like the opening of a flower at first light. It comes with a lot of trepidations on part of the flower and some needed motivation from the rays of the sun. But nonetheless, the outcome is glorious dawn, swaying flowers, flowing breeze. So is the unveiling of hidden talents. Often they are accompanied by hesitation and sometimes with forceful urgings they can result in something beautiful.

Morning Buds is a collection of poems produced after such hesitations and constant urgings. They are created by a group of talented young men who came forth with their ideas, jotted down on paper, with the hope of appealing to an invisible reader. The difference between reading and writing is that the reader rarely goes in blind. They have the author's biography pasted onto some book or website presented to them before they go in to make head or tail of a piece of writing. That is not so when it comes to the writer. The writer has no idea who it is that will pick up their work and how they are going to receive it. A writer's writing is subject to criticism and interpretations a writer is often not made aware of. For these young men to have volunteered their writing for the scrutiny of the world is a brave thing to do as much it is noble.

Writing is a noble profession. You permit strangers into your deepest, most personal thoughts, making them feel privileged without knowing whether or not they are deserving of it. Just as the heavenly Father showers rain on both the good and the wicked, the writer pours out his heart. These young writers too have presented the same without thought and deserve commendation for not just their talent but also their courage and benevolence.

Anavah Moses

(Author and Poet)

Preface

Towards the middle of 2021, urged by a teacher, a group of students started a practice of daily writing. That led to the development of a group called "Teen English". The group lasted only a few months because of the pressure of studies and for a lack of management. What it left behind was a group of children eager to write. It is only deemed fit that the same group of students would come together to greet a farewell to 2021 in the most poetic way possible and greet 2022 in a fragrant manner.

Morning Bud is a collection of poems taken from these boys, some old and some new, aimed at welcoming the New Year with a poetic expression of their hearts.

Taukir Suhan

Taukir Suhan a person who loves creativity and writing poems. He is a student of a reputed English medium school in Kolkata, studying in the eighth standard.

The Fair

So today I decided to go to a fair nearby,

I was alone, but not lonely,

Because watching the children,

Smile and laugh, made me feel like,

I'm living a second childhood

Looking at their triumphant smiles,

Lit up the light within me.

It was an exotic escapade,

A magical delirium,

Which caught me in a euphoria of myself

After all these years, it all came back to me,

The different memories of summer,

All the bittersweet nostalgia,

Cascading dreams, chasing dandelions,

The yummy candies from childhood,

And the beautiful colours of sunset.

But then, a light beaconed me,
From the midst of an abyss,
In the shadows I saw,
My worst nightmare,
An abandoned merry go round,
And all round was dappled darkness,
In that moment, I felt frozen,
My body caught a chill, I started shivering,
And my skin turned pale.
Those moments of stillness
Brought many flashbacks
Of my shredded memories,
Years go by, yet, I remember it all too well.
The bleeding palms, scars on mind,
The wounds on my soul, dreary dreams,
And blood; crimson as murder on a holy day.

That day in my life, was the worst one,

I think I had experienced a little death,

And the only hope was left in a Pandora's box

I was in detrimental dispair, with hollow hope,

But to the doctor who saved me,

I could say a 100 thank yous.

A horrifying accident which I barely survived,

Because, I sat on a broken seat,

Which made me fall,

From the fast moving merry go round.

I never knew that such a simple looking, music playing,

Merry go round, could be so dangerous.

The accident changed my life completely,

I remember, that the doctor told me,

"You are lucky to be alive"

And that was when,

I truly started living my life.

Generation Gap

Many talk about the gap,

the gap between the generations.

The old one's,

find the young one's ignorant and arrogant,

The young one's thinking big and radical, willing to change the world,

finds the old one's odd,

impractical and old fashioned.

But neither is right and neither is wrong.

Cause each generation has it's own time and its own battle,

but in the end each generation

is on the search for peace,

truth and love.

So the generation gap only exists in our minds not in the world.

90s vs 20s

Elders have smiling face,

Youngers have smiling emojis;

Elders are players,

Youngers are gamers;

Elders are listeners,

Youngers are watchers;

Elders are silent,

Youngers are alone;

Elders are seekers,

Youngers are annoyers;

Elders are talkers,

Youngers are chatters;

Elders passed on the pain,

Youngers are crossed the pain;

Elders live in the music,

Youngers enjoy the music;

Beyond everything,

They met in this;

Elders teaches the way of life,

Youngers shows the moment of life.

Childhood memories

The golden period of our life, yes it's our childhood.

We play, eat, study, enjoy, sleep, grow, and form our base of life.

We walk and rise with grade 1 to grade 10 of schooling.

We become a human of identity with of foundation building.

It brings the most fun & frolic times of our life,

As we love to rise and fall in all our endeavours.

Taking part in every competition is our attitude

And making masti by teasing others is our style.

We earn medals and certificates which bring us greater joys.

We get toffees and gifts in our daily chores from seniors.

It's the age of receiving love, care and blessing of parents all the time,

It's the period of becoming one with god.

Smile

A smile is quite a funny thing.

It wrinkles up your face.

And when it's gone

you'll never find

It's seen hiding place.

But for more wonderful it is

To see what smiles can do.

You smile at once one,

He smiles at you,

And so one smile makes two

Rochishnu Majumder

Rochishnu Majumder is a student from St. Lawrence High School. Presently at Class 9, he likes to pen down his imaginations and thoughts from a tender age. Besides writing, he's is fond of reading storybooks and books of knowledge.

Fly Away Bird

Fly away bird, you fly In the limitless, ineffable sky,

Time has come for you to rise high

Fly away bird, you fly.

Your once fragile wings have sturdily grown

Your innocent and tender days you have shown;

Now, glancing high, spread out your wings,

Your aspirations are dragged by the sky kings.

There shall be deliberate attempts to ruin yours' fate,

As your competitors are broiling with jealousy and hate!

They shall try their fullest to cast a gloom on you

For well-wishers in this world are few.

But let these undesirable trials be only unfulfilled hopes

Untie yourself from the nemesis ropes;

Your gloomed mind may be the stepping stone

Of a hued desire, for you to remain to be flown;

Otherwise, it may be a stumbling stone

Of a further anguish, where light shall never be shown.

Let not temporary glistened tears be an everlasting cry,

Fly away bird, you fly high.

The Maze

I'm entangled in a complex maze,

Bewildered people after me they chase,

Dishonesty of some shatter my belief

While others' sincerity gives me relief.

Population in this maze has grown

But a solitary feeling makes me alone;

Although the maze's desolate part

Has people that pleases my heart.

This maze is a crowded public stage,

Some are free, while some are in the cage

People spending lives to sacrifice

But still cannot afford a grain of rice!

Hordes of guilty people, here, intend to lie;

Whereas innocent humans cease to die,

Wonder why there are weapons in children's hands,

Why trust and faith gradually fade in the sand!

There are no bounds for betrayals in this place

Shimmering masks disguise the crooked face,

This maze is an insolvable net throughout the land

Where people's minds I cannot understand.

Inexplicable Sentiment

The boy has got a remote-control toy,
His visage filled with glee and joy ;
He's felicity makes him hop and play
Shimmering like the beam of the day.
From the murky sky like the advent of rain shower,
Like in the gloomy night the fragrant jasmine flower
He seemed to be an innocent infant in mother's lap;
After a hardcore day, like a tranquil nap .
His blissful mind makes him rejoice,
Sweet tunes enmeshing from his voice
All the way to home he sings,
Similar to birds flapping their wings .
It was his father from whom the toy he got ,
The joyful boy thanked him a lot ;
His excitement made him fall and hurt

The toy seemed to be shabby in dirt .

The boy's ears exposed to an evanescent clatter

His posture motionless as his toy shatter;

Unending tears finding no room to enroll,

Sorrow persistent in his innocent soul .

He mourned and remained to weep

His emotions inexplicable and deep;

His doleful cries gathered the crowd,

The azure sky got hidden by the dark cloud.

The Inflamed Spirit

A tiny bird stumped down from a banyan tree

Pain broke his mellifluous dream and let it free;

Blood was protruding from her distorted frame,

It formed a restful fluid bed in her name.

The trivial movements that she made

Were desperate attempts to let agony fade,

The least chirps that sounded from her throat

On a freezing ocean was like a life boat .

The desires in the irregular blinks of her eye

Were trials to not let her spirits die

Pain got stricken in her pretty face,

But inflamed the core of her heart's grace!

Her soul seeking pleasure from the cool breeze,

Pardon begged by the rustling of the banyan trees;

Agony freed the bird from incessant torture

And offered some relief to the little creature.

Pain apologized for this deliberate mishap,

And let the bird rest in death's eternal lap.

An Ideal World

Where people's cries you would not hear,

In none's eyes you shall find tear

From felicity people do not deprive,

Love and affection in this world shall thrive.

Where, from diseases and epidemics people do not expire,

To attain knowledge people always aspire,

Children ignited with inspiring dream

With prosperity the society might gleam.

Where minds exposed to creativity and art

Unleashing imaginations from the heart,

Placidity succeeding over torment and afflict,

World freed of enmity and conflict.

Where nature's allure is intense divine

From all toxics the air it refine,

A world where tranquility and purity we find

That soothes the existing mankind.

Where people's elation you cannot measure,

I would like to live in that world with pleasure

A place which is infilled with unending bliss

An ideal world for me it is.

Arghadeep Das

Arghadeep Das is a student of class 9 studying at St. Lawrence High School. He lives near Jadavpur in Kolkata. He has started writing poems recently motivated by one of his favourite teachers and his parents. Though he didn't write poems earlier he used to recite poems very eagerly. Now he loves to write poems and has gotten extremely engrossed in poetry. Apart from this, he is also interested to know many things mostly about science. He likes to read stories of Sherlock Holmes and Feluda. He is very fond of music and drawing and is very passionate about cricket as well.

Key to Success

If you're one of them who repeatedly tries,
Then you'll surely see your success with your eyes.
Your day will definitely come
If you toil hard and never succumb.

If you've real dedication towards something,
Then you must remember one thing -
That nothing can stop you to achieve victory
And you will surely meet a good destiny.

Hurdles will always be there on the road,
But you can cross those by being bold.
The more obstacles you overcome -
The more stronger you become.

You must always have to be optimistic,

As there is no time to be ominous and pessimistic.

Don't let struggle and depression affect yourself,

Since you can only be successful if you believe in yourself.

The Nocturnal Drama

In the middle of the night
Sweeps past a vision of light,
As I see images in my mind
Where I'm myself of a different kind.

For a minute or two I tend to forget
That what I see is not my hamlet.
I can feel the objects revealing
But just can't control the things.

Just then a lustrous spark jolts me awake
And as I perceive it a dream my mind is berserk
Wondering how good it would have been
If I could be there again at the scene.

The Spring

After the long months of chilly winter,
Comes the spring to provide sweet pleasure.
It helps to ignite the gloomy sun,
With dices to throw to bring out some fun.

Flowers blossom with their charming appearance
Realising a heady and enchanting fragrance.
Trees grow new tender leaves,
The dew drops encrusting all the trees.

The birds soaring high with great elation,
And butterflies roam around with exhilaration.
Fawns and cubs are dancing happily,
As the cuckoo birds sing jovially.

With all its alluring beauty nature smiles.

This is how spring entertains us in its own styles.

My Mom - My Idol

You're the one to bring me up
You're the person to draw my shape,
You are the one to lift me up;
You were the first to see me gape.

To date maybe you're the most remarkable
Whose hands are just tireless,
How you pampered me was extremely adorable;
You're the one who taught me to be fearless.

The one always motivated me
Who inspired me with knowledge,
I thank you for exalting care you give me
You're the best - is what should acknowledge.

I'm always proud to be yours

I'm very lucky to have a mother like you,

You've shared everything that was yours;

There are very few in this world like you.

I know you're always beside me

You are the first to help me in my troubles,

You've devoted your life and love to me;

And finally became the root of my success.

The Blue Expanse

You are so vast as it has no limits,

On which the sun reflects and glints

Your beauty have captured a great part of the world

Which I had always loved and cherished .

You display extreme peace and tranquility -

And sometimes also become boisterous and fiery,

And provides us with an ample water supply;

Above whom the seagulls soar high.

With every single drop of water you form a huge entity

This is how you teach the principal of unity

Showing a great example of freedom

Your endless beauty enlightens my mind when I'm in boredom.

You give shelter to so many marine animals

And ensure that they're not thwarted of their dreams

You give valuables like corals and shells

And a lot of mysteries thou tell.

Subarno Sen

Subarno Sen is a boy from Howrah and a student of the eighth standard in St. Lawrence High School

Tribute to Corona Warriors

Doctor's

Work Day and Night,

Hard and hard

To rescue humankind;

From the Corona pandemic.

Many of them have lost their lives.

But they have not lost, their sight.

Of rescuing the world;

From the virus.

They are doing their duty.

And we should also

Help them,

By doing our duty.

That is to

Wear masks and sanitise ourselves.

For their selfless works.

We should salute them

By saying,

'Ordinary humans, Extraordinary Humanity'.

Online Classes

The world has changed,

From the time;

The Corona arrived.

The schools have

Been transformed,

To e-school.

I mean

The bedrooms,

Have been converted

Into classrooms.

Instead, of the blackboard;

The teachers,

Now uses the;

Presentations and PDFs!

There is no enjoyment,

As, neither the classrooms

Nor, playgrounds

Are there.

I miss

My friends and

Our teachers

So we shall pray,

To God For rescuing,

All of us;

From the pandemic.

And thereby letting

The government,

To resume

The Offline classes.

Life

Life is full of,

Joy and despair.

There are times;

When we suffer.

But we should not

Give up hope.

As we all,

Should remember

Nothing is Impossible.

We should not,

Look back into The past.

And stay busy,

With it.

As,

The thing

That is gone is gone.

Time,

Never waits;

For anybody.

You have to

Stay in pace,

With time.

But, never

Give up. As there are;

More than one ways,

To reach the same Goal.

The Beautiful Night

Dark Night - Dark Night !

The stars are shining brightly .

Over the deep woods ,

Hung over a little mist .

The moon beams make a picturesque scene ;

The dark night and the moon beam look like- '

Candlelight in dark' .

The candlelight denotes the one who succeeds .

In the race of education and humanity .

How educative the dark night is !

Rishav Mitra

Rishav Mitra studies in class 9. He is a huge football freak. He likes to write proses and prompts. He also likes to draw and listen to music.

Christmas

People counting in the midnight hours,

For the Christmas to come along riding on the sleigh.

After the whitewash of the snowfall,

Comes the Christmas day.

Kids waiting eagerly for their present.

And the roasted turkey waiting for them for Thanksgiving.

The taste of the meat is quite pleasant.

As the mischievous things kids do are worth forgiving.

The Witch

When the witch kneel to pray

It's likely to be the end of the day.

The burnt villa starts to kindle,

For the priests, it's likely to be a riddle.

The spirits trapped with the curses,

There is agony fear in the churches.

The corpses are rising alive.

They are like zombies, to the people's surprise.

A bolt of huge lightning struck the banyan tree.

Letting all the cursed souls go free.

The Beauty of the Night

In the dead of the night rises the dazzling moon,

After the rain showers in the month of June.

The sound of the crickets singing in the dark.

Dewdrop collected on the plants in the park.

Owl stalking its prey from the tall trees,

In the forest floor could be heard the crackling of leaves.

Here comes the sun after the end if the night.

The owl comes out victorious after giving a hell of a fight.

List of Contributors

Arghadeep Das

Rishav Mitra

Rochishnu Majumder

Subarno Sen

Taukir Suhan

www.ingramcontent.com/pod-product-compliance
Lightning Source LLC
LaVergne TN
LVHW050425160726
843469LV00041B/1224

* 9 7 8 9 3 5 5 5 9 1 4 2 5 *